LATINITAS MEMORABILIS

LATIN FOR LIVING, LOVING, LEARNING AND LAUGHING

by

John Sullivan

apocryphile press
BERKELEY, CA

Apocryphile Press
1700 Shattuck Ave #81
Berkeley, CA 94709
www.apocryphile.org

Printed in the United States of America
ISBN 9781940671550

Illustrations by Rickard Stenberg

LATINITAS MEMORABILIS

LATIN FOR LIVING, LOVING, LEARNING AND LAUGHING

by

John Sullivan

the apocryphile press
BERKELEY, CA
www.apocryphile.org

CONTENTS

Introduction 07

Pars Prima..11
Latin Sayings, Wisdom of the
Ancients and the Not So Ancient

Pars Secunda..35
Translations into Latin
of Sayings in English from
Myself and Others

About the Author 58

INTRODUCTION

Fratres Sororesque (Brothers and Sisters),

This book originated as the "Latin for the Week" that I added to the announcements I made at the Sunday Service of Unity of Berkeley. The reaction to it was surprisingly positive.

For some people it reminded them of their high school days when they enjoyed Latin. Others thought it was just amusing. Then it became a weekly e-mail to friends and associates throughout the San Francisco Bay Area and elsewhere.

Now I present it to you with both Latin sayings with an English translation and English sayings with a Latin translation. The Latin will always appear first. Some of you may want to cover the English to see if you can translate the Latin, yourself. That's one way to have fun with this book.

You will notice that there are more translations into Latin than out of that language. That's because it is more fun for me that way and more of a challenge.

Since I was born and raised in the Roman Catholic Church, Latin had been with me since the time a priest poured water on me and said, "Ego te baptizo . . ." Every Sunday there was a whole lot of Latin in church including "Hoc est enim corpus meum" said by the priest leaning over the altar with his back to us.

Then every few weeks in the confessional box I was relieved to hear "Ego te absolvo." During that time Latin didn't interest me much even though the chants were beautiful and the words sounded very solemn.

My interest in Latin was born and grew quickly when I entered the Jesuits' Boston College High School in 1953. The assignments we received to translate the words of famous Roman authors into understandable English got me thinking about the different ways people think and express themselves in different languages. In English and Germanic languages, we jam two nouns together and one functions as an adjective, e.g milkman. In Latin that would be vir lactem advehens, a man bringing milk (if they had that job in those days).

I am very thankful to the four quirky Jesuit priests who put us through our paces, Fathers Kelly, Ruttle, Keane and Power. My large Catholic family was very impressed with my learning. What high school kid doesn't like to impress his elders?

I also noticed that something could be a compliment in one language and an insult in another. An Israeli friend told me about the handbook he got when he joined the army in Israel. It said that following its instruction would make him a *rosh gadol,* a big head, meaning smart. Also the phrase in the Hebrew Bible translated into Latin as mingens ad parietem, one who pisses against the wall, means only a fully mature male.

After high school I entered the Discalced Carmelite religious order. "Discalced" comes from the Latin for "without shoes" which meant we wore sandals even in wintertime. We did wear socks in winter but they really weren't warm enough, especially in Wisconsin.

I had three more years of Latin with Father Conrad Fliess who used the "direct method" speaking only Latin in class. We, the students, were cajoled into also speaking Latin to each other. Imagine the awkward fun we had trying to describe modern inventions like airplanes and televisions.

My classmate in those days, Reginald Foster, corresponded with the Latinist for the Pope and later took over that position. He became known for giving tours of the Latin graffiti in Rome, including the sexy stuff. You can see him being interviewed in the film *Religulous* by Bill Maher.

A quote in this book from the biblical Book of Kings about Elijah and Elisha reminds me of Conrad and Reginald. Look for it. My thanks go to Conrad and Reginald.

I must also thank all those who have enjoyed my forays into the language of the ancient Romans and encouraged me, especially my wife Pat, my publisher John Mabry and my fellow lover of Latin and Gregorian chant, Howard Curtis. I must also give a tip of the hat to J.K. Rowling who has helped revive interest in Latin through the spells of the Harry Potter books. *Gratias tibi ago Regina artium magicarum* (Thank you, Queen of the magic arts).

Pars Prima

Latin Sayings, Wisdom of the Ancients and the Not so Ancient

St. Augustin's description of God:

SEMPER AGENS, SEMPER QUIETUS.

Always at work, always at rest.

For those who tend to overextend themselves:

NEMO DAT QUOD NON HABET.

No one gives what he doesn't have.

From the Latin Mass:

SURSUM CORDA.

*Lift up your hearts
(literally "up hearts").*

From my former classmate Reginald Foster

VERBUM SAT SAPIENTI.

A word to the wise is sufficient.

Here's something we might say to ourselves when confronted with a big chocolate cake or a quart of Ben and Jerry's:

FRENA GULAM!

Control your appetite!

My wife Pat and I went to a Laughing Yoga class. It was originated by a medical doctor in India. I was reminded of the following saying:

RISUS OPTIMA MEDICINA EST.

Laughter is the best medicine.

I couldn't find the exact origin of this saying, but there is a saying in the Book of Proverbs: "A glad heart is excellent medicine, a spirit depressed wastes the bones away" (Proverbs 17:22, Jerusalem Bible, English Edition).

AGE QUOD AGIS.

Literally, Do What You Are Doing.
In one word, FOCUS!

Here's a quote from Maximus Syrus (I'm not familiar with him, but I know where he came from, Syria):

REI NULLI PRODEST MORA NISI IRACUNDIAE.

Delay is useful for nothing except anger.

(For those of you who may be studying Latin, I don't know why he chose the two words *rei nulli* instead of *nihil*.)

Here is a old saying
(with an added comment from me):

**ERRARE HUMANUM EST,
IGNOSCERE DIVINUM.**

**SED ALICUI IGNOSCERE QUI
CONTEMPTA EVIDENTIA IN
ERRORE MANET DIFFICILE EST.**

To err is human, to forgive divine.
—Alexander Pope

But it is difficult to forgive someone who
remains in error in spite of the evidence.
—John Sullivan

Here is a well known quote from Terrentius:

HOMO SUM ET NIHIL HUMANI ALIENUM A ME PUTO.

I am a human being and I consider nothing human foreign to me.

Here's another quote I just read from my main man Louis Satchmo Armstrong. When asked how he and his band could be so popular with people all over the world who were so different from each other, he said, *"They're not different as far as we're concerned."* Thank you Terrentius and Pops!

Here is a dialogue from the Latin Vulgate version of the Bible (Vulgate means "for the common people") between Elijah and his number one man, Elisha, just before he took off in his heavenly chariot.

ELIJAH: QUID VIS UT FACIAM TIBI ANTEQUAM TOLLAR A TE?

ELISHA: DA MIHI DUPLICEM PORTIONEM SPIRITUS TUI.

"What do you want me to do for you before I am taken away from you?"

"Give me a double portion of your spirit."

Exactly what every teacher should give to his or her students.

Here' a quote from the famous orator of ancient Rome, Marcus Tullius Cicero. It is from a speech M.T. delivered about a guy in the Senate who was secretly planning to overthrow the government. It can easily be adapted for today's obstructionist politicians.

QUOUSQUE TANDEM ABUTERIS, CATALINA, PATIENTIA NOSTRA?

Just how long will you,
Cataline, abuse our patience?

Here are three ancient short phrases that can be read in both directions. They are palindromes, not that the former governor of Alaska has anything to do with them:

SUM SUMMUS MUS.
AVE EVA. SUMMUS SUMMUS.

I am the greatest mouse.
Hello Eve. We are we are.

A warning counseling caution:

TIMEO DANAOS ET DONA FERENTES.

I fear (not beware of) Greeks bearing gifts.

I hope Dr. Francis of Rome
will lead us on a search for the cure.

DISPUTANDI PRURITUS ECCLESIARUM SCABIES.

***The itch to argue is the skin disease
of the churches.***

As Satchmo would say in agreement,
"Oh, yes!"

Here's a saying some think came from Cicero.
I saw it on an old beat-up van in Berkeley. Even
some old hippies know Latin. This saying is in
no way connected to a former Vice-President of
the U.S.

DUM SPIRO, SPERO.

While I breathe, I have hope.

So never give up.

Here's a common motto taken from the writings of at least two ancient Romans, Seneca and Virgil.

PER ASPERA AD ASTRA.

Through hardships to the stars.

Here's a quote from the Latin translation of the Bible, Book of Proverbs (not a completely accurate translation of the Hebrew but it works for Maya Angelou):

FORTITUDO ET DECOR INDUMENTUM EJUS ET RIDEBIT IN DIE NOVISSIMO.

She is clothed with strength and dignity and will laugh on the final day.

I don't know the author of this.
I think it's appropriate for July 4.

LIBERTAS SUPRA LEVAMENTUM.

Freedom above comfort.

(i.e., don't get too comfortable
with your freedom.)

This quote is from the Latin Vulgate translation of the Bible and from the sexiest book of the Bible, *The Song of Songs.*

LAEVA EJUS SUB CAPITE MEO ET DEXTERA ILLIUS AMPLEXABITUR ME.

His left hand is under my head and his right will embrace me.

For the Latin students among you, I don't know why the Latin translator used both *ejus* and *illius* instead of just one or the other. I'm thankful to the rabbis who considered this book the holiest of the holy books and so preserved it.

Here's a simple statement
from our old Roman friend, Seneca.

RES SEVERA EST VERUM GAUDIUM.

True joy is a serious thing.

Here are two quotes from
Roman writers about laughter:

HORACE: REDENTEM DICERE VERUM QUID VETAT?

*What prohibits a laughing person
from speaking the truth?*
(This makes me think of Jon Stewart.)

CATULLUS: RISU INEPTO RES INEPTIOR NULLA EST.

*Nothing is more inappropriate
than an inappropriate laugh.*

Here's another metaphor
for a common complaint:

ELEPHANTEM E MUSCA FACIS.
You are making an elephant out of a fly.

Here's one of those old sayings that has an equivalent in every language. It shows how much the Romans loved to eat, something inherited by all Italians:

VELOCIUS QUAM ASPARAGI COQUANTUR.

Faster than asparagus is cooked.

(I don't know why they put it in the plural.)

This expresses something
many have experienced:

DOCENDO DISCIMUS.

We learn by teaching.

Another quote from Cicero.

ASSIDUUS USUS USUS UNI REI DEDITUS ET INGENIUM ET ARTEM SAEPE VINCIT.

Constant practice given to one thing often surpasses natural ability and skill.

So keep at it, you can probably do it.

Two sayings encouraging
moderation and balance:

IN MEDIO STAT VIRTUS.
EXTREMA SE TANGUNT.

Virtue stands in the middle.
The extremes touch each other.

Here's what our alarm clocks
tell us every morning:

Surge et illuminare!

Rise and shine!

Here's a saying related to recent events
from the Roman playwright Juvenal:

Quis custodiet ipsos custodes?

Who will police the police?

Pars Secunda

Translations Into Latin of Sayings in English from Myself and Others

SILENTIUM AUREUM EST, SED ALIQUANDO STREPITUM FACERE DEBEMUS.

Silence is golden, but sometimes we have to make noise.

This proverb about golden silence perhaps dates to ancient Egypt. I added the part about sometimes having to make noise.

ESTO HIC NUNC. ESTO ALICUBI POSTEA. QUID DIFICILE IN HAC RE?

Be here now, be somewhere else later.
What's so difficult about that?

—David Bader

Potestas Spiritualis
Musicae Fovet Pacem.

The spiritual power of music fosters peace.

Secundum veritatem nostram vivere debemus.

We should live according to our truth.

Paratus, volens et potens.

Ready, willing and able.

DEO VOLENTE ET RIVO NON SURGENTE.

God willin' and the creek don't rise.

Author unknown. Also unknown if "creek" referred to a body of water or the Native American Creeks. As one saying put it, "God willing and the Creeks don't fire."

ADERO TINTINABULIS INSTRUCTUS.

I'll be there with bells on.

Another proverb with conflicting theories about its origin.

Amator librorum sum. Nonne idem de te dicere possum?

I am a lover of books.
Can't I say the same about you?
—John Sullivan

Matrem terram omnes nos protegere debemus.

We all must protect mother earth.

Advice from Jimmy Durante:

Unaquaeque dies cantu incipienda est etsiamsi res male eveniunt.

You gotta start off each day with a song even when things go wrong.

**FUMOSUS ILLE URSUS DICIT,
"TU SOLUS CONFLAGRATIONES
SYLVESTRES PROHIBERE POTES."**

*Smokey the Bear says,
"Only you can prevent forest fires."
—U.S. Forest Services 1944 ad campaign.*

**ALIQUANDO NOMINA VESTRA
OBLIVISCAR SED NUMQUAM
VOS OBLIVISCAR. SUM QUI SUM
QUIA COGNOVI VOS.**

*Sometimes I will forget your names,
but you yourselves I will never forget.
I am who I am because I knew you.
—Rev. DeeAnn Weir-Morency, adapting a
phrase from the play, Wicked*

GRATIAS AGAMUS PRO DIEBUS PRAETERITIS, VIVAMUS HIC ET NUNC, EXPECTEMUS BONA FUTURA.

Let us give thanks for the past,
live here and now,
look forward to future good things.

In honor of Pete Seeger, Here's my translation of words from a song he often sang to support the struggles for peace and freedom. I think these words will fit the melody. Try it.

SUPERABIMUS, SUPERABIMUS, SUPERABIMUS ALIQUANDO. IMO CORDE CERTE CREDO. SUPERABIMUS ALIQUANDO.

We shall overcome etc.

The famous civil rights song, "We Shall Overcome" is derived from an old hymn by Charles Albert Findley. See how well you can match up the Latin wording with your knowledge of this song!

This may have been literally true
for some in Roman times:

BRACHIO CRUREQUE CONSTAT.

It costs an arm and a leg.
—Author unknown.

This is my translation of a quote from C.H,
Spurgeon, a 19th century preacher and author:

DISCITE DICERE "NON."
MAGIS VOBIS PRODERIT QUAM
INGENIUM LINGUAM
LATINAM LEGENDI.

Learn to say no.
It will be more valuable to you
than the ability to read Latin.

**UNUS AMICUS FIDELIS IDEM
PRETIUM HABET AC DECEM
MILLIA CONSANGUINEI.**

*One faithful friend is worth
ten thousand relatives.
—Euripides*

**ECCE VERBA VIRI QUI TOTA VITA
SUA SERVOS POSSIDEBAT: OMNES
HOMINES AEQUALES CREATI SUNT.**

*Here are the words of a man who owned
slaves his whole life:
All men are created equal.*

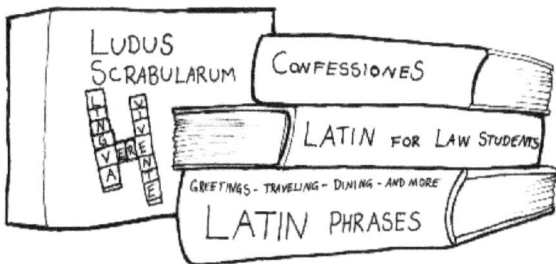

I've been thinking about why I do this. Here is my answer in Latin.

PLACET MIHI MONSTRARE VOBIS QUANTUM GAUDIUM INVENERI POSSIT IN LINGUA VERE VIVENTE.

It pleases me to show you how much joy can be found in a truly living language.

One of my friends asked for Latin about dogs. So here's the first, my translation of something Tom Sienstra, a writer for the *SF Chronicle* wrote:

Nitor aequiparare opinioni quam de me canis meus habet.

I'm trying to live up to the opinion my dog has of me.

Here's something from my yet-to-be-published *Little Book of Cat Wisdom*:

TOTA VITA FELIS IN TRES PARTES DIVISA EST, SCILICET: ESUS, SOMNUS ET LUDUS.

All of a cat's life is divided into three parts, that is: eating, sleeping and playing.

When I imagine us all reading
Latin together, I say this:

TOTA TURBA ADEST!

The gang's all here!
—Traditional song; author unknown.

PERMITTITE ME VOS OBLECTARE ET FORTASSE NOS OMNES ALIQUID NOVI DISCEMUS.

*Let me entertain you and perhaps
we will all learn something new.*

("Let Me Entertain You" is a song by Robbie Williams and Greg Chambers, but I made up the rest of it!)

Here's my translation into Latin of a joke from my friend (the original) Tim McGraw. Thanks Tim!

VIR ROMANUS LOCUM BIBENDI* INTRAT ET DUOS DIGITOS LEVANS DICIT "QUINQUE CERVESIAS SI VIS."

A Roman enters a bar and lifting two fingers says, "Five beers, please."

(I know of no exact word for a bar or saloon. *Locum bibendi* is the best I could do—"a place for drinking." *Taberna* means a small store for food and wine.)

Some good advice from an old
Jesuit retreat master, whose name
I do not recall:

PRESENTIAM DEI RECORDAMINI QUIA NUMQUAM ABEST.

*Call to mind the presence of God
because it is never absent.*

For those of you who are fans of wizardry,
here are three spells (*incantamenta*)
I have concocted:

CICOLATE, POTESTATEM TUAM IN ME DELEO.

Chocolate, I destroy your power over me.

TRANSFORMO CONFUSIONEM IN CLARITATEM.

I transform confusion into clarity.

IRA, NUNC REGO TE ET DIRIGO AD BONUM.

Anger, I now rule and direct you toward the good.

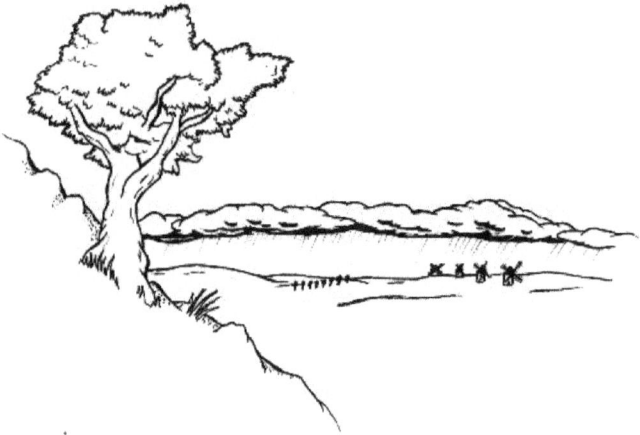

QUANDO COLLOQUIUM MUTAMUS, POSTERITATEM ETIAM MUTAMUS.

When we change the conversation,
we also change the future.
—Juanita Brown

I was translating a saying in English into Latin and recalled a two word Latin quote that says practically the same thing. So here are both of them.

NOLI PROCRASTINARE EA QUAE HODIE AGERE POTES.

Don't put off to tomorrow
what you can do today.
—Credited to Benjamin Franklin
and Thomas Jefferson

CARPE DIEM!

Seize the day.
—Attributed to the Latin poet Horace.

ABOUT THE AUTHOR

As you already know from his introduction, John was a member of the Roman Catholic Church and a priest of that Church for a time. He was born in Boston, MA on Feb. 26 1940 to a firefighter and a housewife. He has lived in Boston, in and near Milwaukee, in Washington, DC and now in Oakland, CA.

After leaving the Church and the priesthood, he married Nancy who introduced him to a world different from that of a religious order. He considers his life since then "a long strange trip" with varied employment, such as security guard and dispatcher as well as indexer and abstractor.

He is now married to Pat McHenry Sullivan who has encouraged his writing and helped him admit after so many years that he is a writer. Thus we have his first published book. Look for his upcoming fantasy novel about Blackfire, the wizard cat.

www.ingramcontent.com/pod-product-compliance
Lightning Source LLC
Chambersburg PA
CBHW070206060426
42445CB00033B/1721